ISO/IEC 17025:2017 and the success of the laboratory: a guide for implementation

Rodrigo Palma

Published by Rodrigo Palma, 2024.

While every precaution has been taken in the preparation of this book, the publisher assumes no responsibility for errors or omissions, or for damages resulting from the use of the information contained herein.

ISO/IEC 17025:2017 AND THE SUCCESS OF THE LABORATORY: A GUIDE FOR IMPLEMENTATION

First edition. April 28, 2024.

Copyright © 2024 Rodrigo Palma.

ISBN: 979-8224186228

Written by Rodrigo Palma.

Also by Rodrigo Palma

El Arte de Guiar desde Adentro: Estrategias para Desarrollar tu Liderazgo Personal

ISO/IEC 17025:2017 and the success of the laboratory: a guide for implementation

ISO/IEC 17025:2017 y el éxito del laboratorio: una guía para la implementación

The Art of Leading from Within: Strategies to Develop Your Personal Leadership

"ISO/IEC 17025:2017 and the success of the laboratory: a guide for implementation"

RODRIGO R. PALMA MENA

DEDICATION

Dear family,
I want to dedicate this book to all of you, who have been my support and my strength during all this time. Without your love and support, this achievement would not have been possible.
Thank you for your patience, understanding and constant encouragement. Each one of you has been a fundamental pillar in my life and I am grateful to have you in my family.
I hope this achievement inspires each one of you to follow your dreams and goals with dedication and effort. Always remember that the love and support of family is the key to success.
With all my love and gratitude,
Rodrigo R. Palma Mena

CONTENT

THANKS

I, Rodrigo Palma Mena, would like to take this opportunity to express my most sincere gratitude to all the people who have given me their support and help in carrying out this project.

First of all, I want to thank ISO advisor Patricia Gutiérrez for her valuable collaboration and advice in the development of this book. Their experience and knowledge have been essential in achieving the goals we had set for ourselves.

I cannot fail to mention Renato and Sebastián Palma for their constant support and encouragement in moments of doubt and fatigue during the preparation of this book. Thanks to them, I have managed to overcome obstacles and continue forward.

Finally, I thank my family and friends for their understanding and encouragement at all times, and for their confidence in my ability to carry out this project.

To all of them, my most sincere appreciation. This book would not have been possible without your unconditional collaboration and support.

1 INTRODUCTION TO ISO/IEC 17025:2017 STANDARD

The ISO/IEC 17025:2017 standard establishes the requirements for the technical competence, impartiality and quality of testing and calibration laboratories. The objective of this standard is to provide a framework for laboratories to demonstrate their ability to perform reliable and accurate tests and calibrations, and for their results to be internationally accepted.

The purpose of implementing ISO/IEC 17025:2017 in a testing or calibration laboratory is to provide a systematic framework for quality management and technical competence, enabling laboratories to demonstrate their ability to perform tests and calibrations. reliable and accurate. The standard establishes requirements for the organizational structure, the management of resources, the testing and calibration process, the handling of the results and the continuous improvement of the quality management system of the laboratory.

Implementation of ISO/IEC 17025:2017 can provide several benefits to a testing or calibration laboratory. First, implementation of the standard can help improve the quality and reliability of test and calibration results, which can improve customer satisfaction and the reputation of the laboratory. In addition, the implementation of the standard can help laboratories improve the efficiency and effectiveness of their processes and reduce errors and non-conformities. It can also provide a strong foundation for cooperation and international recognition of test and calibration results, which can be especially important for laboratories that perform tests and calibrations for international customers.

The ISO/IEC 17025:2017 standard is applied in a wide variety of contexts in which laboratories perform tests and calibrations, including the food, pharmaceutical, chemical, materials, and other industries. For example, in the food industry, laboratories can use ISO/IEC

17025:2017 to demonstrate their ability to perform food quality tests, such as nutrient content, allergen detection, and food safety assessment. . In the pharmaceutical industry, laboratories can use ISO/IEC 17025:2017 to demonstrate their ability to perform quality drug testing, such as impurity identification and potency assessment. In the chemical industry, laboratories can use ISO/IEC 17025:2017 to demonstrate their ability to perform quality tests on chemicals, such as chemical composition determination and toxicity assessment. In the materials industry, laboratories can use ISO/IEC 17025:2017 to demonstrate their ability to perform quality tests on materials, such as determination of mechanical properties and evaluation of durability. In summary, the ISO/IEC 17025:2017 standard is applicable to any laboratory that performs tests and calibrations and that wishes to demonstrate its technical capacity and its commitment to quality and continuous improvement.

The ISO/IEC 17025:2017 standard establishes the general requirements for the technical competence and quality management of testing and calibration laboratories. The standard is based on two fundamental pillars: the technical competence of the personnel and the quality of the processes and management.

The structure of the standard is divided into two main sections: section 4, which establishes the quality system management requirements, and section 5, which establishes the technical requirements for carrying out tests and calibrations.

Section 4 includes general requirements for organizational structure, human resources, document management, records management, equipment and infrastructure management, process management, and continuous improvement.

Section 5 includes the technical requirements for performing tests and calibrations, such as validation of test methods, traceability of measurements, uncertainty of measurements, selection and calibration of equipment, and management of results. Of the tests.

ISO/IEC 17025:2017 is closely related to ISO 9001:2015, which sets out the requirements for a more general quality management system. Although ISO/IEC 17025:2017 focuses on quality management and technical competence of testing and calibration laboratories, it can be successfully integrated with other management systems, such as ISO 9001:2015 and ISO 14001:2015.. Integration of ISO/IEC 17025:2017 with other management systems can help improve the efficiency and effectiveness of laboratory processes and reduce redundancy in system management.

In summary, ISO/IEC 17025:2017 is an important framework for quality management and technical competence in testing and calibration laboratories. The standard establishes detailed requirements for the organizational structure and management of resources, as well as for carrying out tests and calibrations. Additionally, the standard can be successfully integrated with other management systems, which can improve the efficiency and effectiveness of laboratory processes.

The following chapters of the book would cover in detail the specific requirements of ISO/IEC 17025:2017 and how to implement them in a test or calibration laboratory. In these chapters, readers will find detailed information on the technical and management requirements of the standard, as well as practical examples and useful advice for its implementation in the laboratory.

This book can be used by professionals in charge of implementing ISO/IEC 17025:2017 in their laboratory as a useful tool to achieve a successful and efficient implementation. The chapters are designed to provide a detailed understanding of the requirements of the standard and how to meet them in practice. In addition, the book would include practical examples, templates, and useful tips to help practitioners implement the standard effectively. In summary, this book would be a valuable tool for any laboratory seeking to implement ISO/IEC 17025:2017 and improve its quality management and technical competence.

2 STRUCTURE OF THE QUALITY MANAGEMENT SYSTEM: ISO/IEC 17025:2017

The ISO/IEC 17025:2017 standard establishes the requirements for technical competence and quality management in testing and calibration laboratories. The implementation of a quality management system is essential to comply with the requirements of the standard.

The structure of the quality management system is divided into two main sections: management and technical.

The management section sets out the requirements for quality management and laboratory management. It includes the definition of the laboratory's quality policy, the identification of risks and opportunities associated with the testing and calibration services offered by the laboratory, the management of resources (human, financial, material, etc.), the management of documents and records, non-conformity management, continuous improvement and management review.

The technical section establishes the requirements for the test and calibration process, including the selection, validation and verification of test and calibration methods, sample management, calibration and maintenance of test and calibration equipment, evaluation of measurement uncertainty, quality assurance of test and calibration results, reporting and technical record keeping.

Resource management includes the management of personnel, equipment, infrastructure, work environment and finances, and explains how these resources should be managed to ensure that the organization has the necessary resources to meet the requirements of the standard.

Document and record management is an important component of the quality management system, which describes how documentation and records should be managed to ensure traceability, confidentiality and availability of the information necessary to meet the requirements of the rule.

Risk and opportunity management is a key practice of quality management and explains how risk should be managed in the laboratory to prevent or mitigate risks and seize opportunities for quality improvement.

Nonconformity management is another key quality management practice and describes how nonconformities should be managed to identify, correct, and prevent their recurrence.

Finally, continuous improvement is a fundamental process in quality management and it explains how the continuous improvement process should be managed to ensure that the organization is constantly evolving and improving its performance and compliance with the requirements of the standard.

INDEX STANDARD ISO/IEC 17025:2017

3 GENERAL REQUIREMENTS FOR TECHNICAL COMPETENCE AND IMPARTIALITY OF LABORATORIES

ISO/IEC 17025:2017 establishes the general requirements for the technical competence and impartiality of testing and calibration laboratories. Some of the general requirements include:

1. Competent personnel: The laboratory must have competent personnel in terms of education, training and experience, to carry out the required tests and calibrations.

2. Documented procedures: The laboratory must have documented procedures to carry out the testing and calibration activities, as well as to manage the quality system of the laboratory.

3. Equipment and materials: The laboratory must have the appropriate equipment and materials to carry out the tests and calibrations, and they must be calibrated and verified regularly.

4. Traceability: The laboratory must establish and maintain the traceability of the measurements made.

5. Quality control: The laboratory must implement measures to control the quality of test and calibration results, including participation in proficiency testing programs and the implementation of internal controls.

6. Document Management: The laboratory must establish and maintain a document management system to ensure that procedures are up to date and accessible to personnel.

7. Impartiality: The laboratory must implement measures to guarantee impartiality in all activities, including the management of conflicts of interest and the protection of confidentiality.

8. Review of the management system: The laboratory must carry out a review of the quality management system periodically to ensure that

it complies with the requirements established in the standard and to identify opportunities for improvement.

These are just some of the general requirements established by ISO/IEC 17025:2017 to ensure the technical competence and impartiality of testing and calibration laboratories. It is important to note that these requirements may vary depending on the specific applicable regulations and the characteristics of the laboratory in question.

ISO/IEC 17025:2017 is made up of two main sections: Section 4, which sets out the general requirements for the technical competence of laboratories, and Section 5, which sets out the requirements for impartiality and confidentiality.

In Section 4, specific requirements are established for personnel, equipment and materials, measurement traceability, quality control, document management, and management system review. For example, in terms of personnel, the laboratory is required to have personnel who are competent in terms of education, training, and experience, and that these personnel participate in ongoing training and development programs. As for the equipment and materials, it is required that they be regularly calibrated and verified, and that adequate quality controls be implemented to guarantee that the results are accurate and reliable.

In Section 5, specific requirements are established to ensure impartiality and confidentiality in all laboratory activities. For example, the laboratory is required to establish and maintain an impartiality policy and to manage conflicts of interest effectively. The laboratory is also required to implement measures to ensure the confidentiality of test and calibration results, and to protect the intellectual property and data of its customers.

In addition to the general requirements established by ISO/IEC 17025:2017, laboratories are also required to undergo periodic audits to assess their compliance with the requirements of the standard. These audits are carried out by independent accreditation bodies, which assess the technical competence and impartiality of the laboratory. Depending on the results of the audit, the laboratory can be accredited or not accredited to carry out tests and calibrations according to the standard.

4 PLANNING THE IMPLEMENTATION OF ISO/IEC 17025:2017

The implementation of the ISO /IEC 17025:2017 standard requires proper planning and a clear strategy to ensure that all the requirements of the standard are met. Here are some steps to plan implementation of the standard:

1. Familiarize yourself with the standard: The first step is to become familiar with the ISO /IEC 17025:2017 standard and understand all its requirements. The standard can be purchased on the ISO website or through certification and consulting bodies.

2. Identify areas for improvement: After learning about the standard, an initial evaluation of the laboratory must be carried out to identify areas that need improvement. This may involve reviewing existing procedures, equipment and materials, personnel, quality controls, and documentation.

3. Create an implementation team: It is important to create an implementation team for the standard, which is made up of laboratory personnel with knowledge and experience in the quality area and who have the time and resources necessary to carry out the project.

4. Develop an action plan: Once areas for improvement have been identified, the implementation team should develop an action plan to address each of the standard's requirements. This plan should include clear goals, timelines, responsibilities, and resources needed to implement each requirement.

5. Conduct training and education: It is important that all laboratory personnel receive adequate training and education in the requirements of the standard and how to implement them. This may involve internal or external training, training courses and workshops.

6. Implement the action plan: Once the action plan has been developed and staff have received appropriate training, implementation

of the action plan can begin. This may involve updating procedures, purchasing new equipment and materials, implementing quality controls, and reviewing documentation.

7. Carry out internal audits: It is important to carry out periodic internal audits to assess the laboratory's compliance with the requirements of the standard. This can help identify areas that need improvement and correct any issues prior to the certification audit.

8. Get certified: Finally, the laboratory can apply for ISO/IEC 17025:2017 certification through accredited certification bodies. The certification audit will assess the laboratory's compliance with the requirements of the standard and, if met, certification will be granted. It is important to take into account that the certification must be renewed periodically through follow-up audits.

It is important to highlight that the process of obtaining ISO/IEC 17025:2017 accreditation can be long and expensive, but it is essential to demonstrate the technical competence and the quality of the services offered by the laboratory.

5 RESOURCE MANAGEMENT FOR THE IMPLEMENTATION OF THE ISO/IEC 17025:2017 STANDARD

For the implementation of the ISO / IEC 17025:2017 standard, it is important to have a resource management plan that allows the efficient and effective use of available resources. Below is a resource management plan that can be adapted to the specific needs of each laboratory:

1. Identify the resources needed: The first step is to identify the resources needed to implement the standard, including personnel, equipment, materials, training, and documentation.

2. Assign responsibilities: It is important to assign clear responsibilities to each member of the implementation team to ensure that resources are used effectively. This may involve assigning specific tasks and setting deadlines for their completion.

3. Assess the capacity of staff: It is important to assess the capacity of existing staff to meet the requirements of the standard. This may involve assessing technical skills, experience and knowledge in the area of quality.

4. Identify training needs: After assessing staff capacity, training needs must be identified to ensure that staff have the knowledge and skills necessary to implement the standard. This may involve conducting internal or external training and allocating resources to cover training costs.

5. Evaluate existing equipment and materials: It is important to evaluate existing equipment and materials to determine if they meet the requirements of the standard. This may involve evaluating the calibration and maintenance of equipment and identifying missing equipment or materials.

6. Acquire new equipment and materials: If missing equipment or materials are identified, it is important to acquire them to ensure that the

requirements of the standard are met. This may involve the allocation of resources for the acquisition of new equipment and materials.

7. Establish a quality control system: It is important to establish a quality control system to ensure that test results are accurate and reliable. This may involve evaluating and updating existing procedures, implementing quality controls, and allocating resources for quality control testing.

8. Guarantee the availability of the necessary documentation: It is important to guarantee that all the necessary documentation is available and updated. This may involve allocating resources to update existing procedures and documentation.

9. Carry out monitoring and evaluation: It is important to carry out regular monitoring and evaluation to ensure that resources are being used effectively and to identify areas that need improvement. This may involve conducting internal audits, evaluating customer satisfaction, and allocating resources for continuous improvement.

In general, a resource management plan for the implementation of the ISO / IEC 17025:2017 standard must be flexible and adapt to the specific needs of each laboratory. By following these steps, the laboratory can ensure that it is effectively using available resources and meeting the requirements of the standard.

6 ESTABLISHMENT OF A QUALITY MANAGEMENT SYSTEM TO COMPLY WITH ISO/IEC 17025:2017

The quality policy is the starting point for the implementation of the quality management system, establishing, communicating and reviewing the quality policy is essential to ensure that the organization is committed to continuous improvement and compliance with the requirements of the standard. ISO/ /IEC 17025:2017. The quality policy must be developed and established, communicated to all levels of the organization and periodically reviewed to ensure its relevance and effectiveness.

The specific requirements of the standard are addressed, including the need for the policy to be consistent with the objectives of the organization, to commit to compliance with legal and regulatory requirements, and to promote continual improvement in all aspects of the operation. from the laboratory.

In addition, the quality policy can be used as a means to engage and motivate laboratory personnel, and it must be communicated effectively to ensure that all members of the organization understand its importance and their role in its compliance.

It is also necessary to execute the best practices for the review of the quality policy, including the importance of establishing clear and measurable objectives and goals, and the need to carry out periodic reviews to ensure their adequacy and effectiveness.

Example of Quality Policy:
"At [name of laboratory], we are committed to delivering accurate and reliable test and calibration results that meet the requirements of

our customers and applicable international standards. To achieve this, we commit to:

Maintain and continually improve our quality management system to ensure technical competence and excellence in service provision.

Provide our staff with the necessary education and training to improve their technical competence and interpersonal skills, and encourage their active participation in continuous improvement.

Identify and manage the risks and opportunities associated with our activities and services to minimize negative impacts and maximize benefits for our clients, our staff and the environment.

Comply with applicable legal and regulatory requirements, as well as the requirements of ISO/IEC 17025:2017 and other relevant international standards.

Satisfy and exceed the expectations of our customers through constant communication and dialogue and continuous improvement of our services.

This quality policy is reviewed and updated annually to ensure its relevance and adequacy."

To efficiently establish a quality management system to comply with ISO/IEC 17025:2017, it is recommended to follow the following steps:

1. Know the ISO / IEC 17025:2017 standard: It is important to know in detail the requirements of the standard in order to establish a plan that meets its specifications.

2. Carry out a diagnosis: A diagnosis of the current system must be carried out to identify the strengths and weaknesses. This analysis can be carried out by a specialized consultant or by the organization's internal team.

3. Establish an action plan: Based on the results of the diagnosis, an action plan must be established to comply with the requirements of the

standard. This plan must include clear objectives, deadlines, responsible parties and necessary resources.

4. Establish a quality manual: A quality manual must be established that describes the procedures, policies and requirements of the ISO / IEC 17025: 2017 standard. This manual should be regularly reviewed and updated.

5. Establish Documented Procedures: Documented procedures should be established for all activities that affect the quality of test and calibration results. These procedures must be clear, precise and easily understandable.

6. Establish a document control system: A document control system must be established to ensure the correct identification, review and approval of all documents necessary for quality management.

7. Establish a record control system: A record control system should be established to ensure proper identification, storage, and disposition of test and calibration records.

8. Establish an education and training plan: An education and training plan must be established for the personnel involved in the tests and calibrations. This plan must ensure that all personnel have the necessary knowledge and skills to carry out their work effectively and comply with the requirements of the standard.

9. Establish an internal audit plan: An internal audit plan must be established to ensure the correct implementation and maintenance of the quality management system.

10. Carry out a final evaluation: Finally, a final evaluation must be carried out to verify that the quality management system meets the requirements of ISO / IEC 17025:2017 and that it is being implemented effectively.

By following these steps, a quality management system can be established that meets the requirements of ISO /IEC 17025:2017 and ensures the quality of test and calibration results.

Below is a template for creating a quality manual:

1. Introduction
- Presentation of the quality manual
- Objectives and scope of the quality manual
- Applicable regulatory and legal references

2. Quality policy
- Laboratory quality policy statement
- Management commitment to quality and continuous improvement.

3. Organization of the laboratory
- Description of the organizational structure of the laboratory
- Responsibilities and authorities of each function
- Description of key laboratory processes

4. Resource management
- Personnel requirements (competence, training, skills, etc.)
- Equipment management and calibration
- Management of infrastructure and work environment

5. Control of documents and records
- Description of the document management system (creation, review, approval, distribution, etc.)
- Control of records (identification, storage, access, preservation, etc.)

6. Management review
- Description of the management review process of the quality management system
- Review of quality objectives and performance indicators
- Continuous improvement of the quality management system

7. Carrying out tests and /or calibrations
- Description of the processes for carrying out tests and calibrations.

- Operating and technical procedures (methods, techniques, equipment, etc.)
- Validation of methods and procedures

8. Management of non-conformity
- Description of the non-conformity management process and corrective actions.
- Investigation of the root causes and definition of measures to prevent their recurrence.
9. Internal audits
- Description of the internal audit process of the quality management system.
- Planning, carrying out and monitoring of internal audits
- Improvement actions derived from internal audits
10. Evaluation of suppliers and subcontractors
- Description of the supplier and subcontractor evaluation and selection process.
- Management of relationships with suppliers and subcontractors
- Monitoring and evaluation of the performance of suppliers and subcontractors.
11. Security and confidentiality
- Description of the security and confidentiality measures applicable to the laboratory and its clients.
- Protection of confidential customer information and data
12. Annexes
- Glossary of terms
- Record formats and document management formats
- Operating and technical procedures

Remember that this is only a basic template, and that it must be adapted and customized for the specific needs and characteristics of each laboratory. In addition, it is important to ensure that the quality manual meets all the requirements of ISO/IEC 17025:2017 and that it is regularly updated and reviewed to ensure its effectiveness and up-to-date.

7 REQUIREMENTS OF THE ISO/iec 17025:2017 STANDARD FOR THE DOCUMENTATION OF THE QUALITY MANAGEMENT SYSTEM

Regarding the identification of the documents necessary to comply with the requirements of the ISO/IEC 17025:2017 standard, it is important to take into account that the standard requires the existence of a quality manual, documented procedures and records. Documented procedures are those that describe how tests and calibrations are performed, while records are the documents that contain the results of the tests and calibrations performed. In addition, the organization may also need other documents for its own internal use, such as work instructions, forms, etc.

Regarding the document control system, it is important to ensure that a clear process is established for the review and approval of documents, as well as the identification and elimination of obsolete versions. This is especially important to ensure that staff are using the correct version of the documents.

With regard to the record control system, it is important to establish adequate retention periods for the records, taking into account the nature and complexity of the tests and calibrations carried out. It is also important to establish a process for the identification, storage, and disposal of obsolete records.

Regarding the review and update plan, it is important to ensure that realistic deadlines are established and that those responsible for the review and update of documents and records are clearly defined. In addition, it is also important to establish a clear process for the distribution and communication of updated documents and records.

Finally, it is important to highlight that the implementation of a quality management system based on the ISO/IEC 17025:2017 standard not only implies the documentation of the system, but also the implementation of processes and work practices that ensure the quality of the results. of tests and calibrations. Therefore, it is important that the organization takes into account both the documentation of the system and the effective implementation of the same in its day to day.

To comply with the requirements of ISO/IEC 17025:2017 for quality management system documentation, it is recommended to follow the following steps:

1. Know the requirements of the standard: It is important to know in detail the requirements of the ISO / IEC 17025:2017 standard regarding the quality management system documentation.

2. Identify the necessary documents: The documents necessary to comply with the requirements of the standard must be identified. These may include, for example, the quality manual, documented procedures, records, and audit reports.

3. Establish a document control system: A document control system must be established to ensure the correct identification, review and approval of all documents necessary for quality management. This system must include, for example, the assignment of a version number to each document and the definition of those responsible for review and approval.

4. Establish a record control system: A record control system should be established to ensure proper identification, storage, and disposition of test and calibration records. This system must include, for example, the definition of those responsible for the registry and the definition of the conservation periods.

5. Establish a review and update plan: A review and update plan must be established for the documents and records of the quality management system. This plan must include review and update deadlines, responsible parties and procedures for communication and distribution of updated documents and records.

6. Establish a training and training plan: A training and training plan must be established for the personnel involved in the documentation and management of the quality management system. This plan must ensure that all personnel have the necessary knowledge and skills to carry out their work effectively and comply with the requirements of the standard.

7. Carry out a final evaluation: Finally, a final evaluation must be carried out to verify that the quality management system documentation meets the requirements of ISO / IEC 17025:2017 and that it is being implemented effectively.

Here are some examples of how a quality management system based on ISO/IEC 17025:2017 can be effectively implemented:

• Work procedures: The ISO /IEC 17025:2017 standard requires that documented procedures be established that describe how tests and calibrations are performed. For example, in a chemical analysis laboratory, a documented procedure may be established detailing how samples are taken and handled, how tests are performed, and how results are recorded. By effectively implementing these procedures, you ensure that test results are consistent and reliable.

• Internal quality control: The ISO /IEC 17025:2017 standard requires internal quality control processes to be implemented to verify the accuracy and reliability of the tests and calibrations performed. For example, in a materials testing laboratory, an internal quality control process may be implemented that involves regular performance of benchmark tests, review of test records, and implementation of corrective actions in the event that errors are found. detect errors.

• Personnel training: The ISO /IEC 17025:2017 standard requires that personnel involved in carrying out tests and calibrations be trained to ensure that they have the necessary knowledge and skills to carry out their work effectively. For example, in a material testing laboratory, a training plan may be established that includes training in the use of test equipment, interpretation of results, and implementation of internal quality control processes.

• Analysis of results: The ISO /IEC 17025:2017 standard requires that a critical analysis of the results of tests and calibrations be carried out to verify their accuracy and reliability. For example, in a clinical analysis laboratory, a results analysis process can be established that involves the review of the records of the tests performed, the identification of trends and the implementation of corrective measures in case errors or discrepancies are detected. .

These are just a few examples of how a quality management system based on ISO/IEC 17025:2017 can be effectively implemented. In general, the effective implementation of the quality management system involves a combination of documentation, training, implementation of processes and work practices, and critical analysis of the results to ensure the quality of the tests and/or calibrations performed.

8 CONTROLS OF RECORDS FOR THE IMPLEMENTATION OF THE ISO/IEC 17025:2017 STANDARD

The ISO/IEC 17025:2017 standard establishes that laboratories must maintain records documenting all relevant activities and results to ensure the quality and validity of test and calibration results. These records may include test and calibration reports, equipment maintenance and calibration records, personnel training records, internal quality control records, and any other records required by the standard.

Importantly, records are essential for traceability of test and calibration results, and for demonstrating competence and compliance with the requirements of ISO/IEC 17025:2017. The records also allow for the identification and resolution of any problems or nonconformities that may arise in the testing and calibration process.

Therefore, record control is a fundamental requirement of ISO/IEC 17025:2017 and laboratories are expected to establish and maintain an appropriate record control system that ensures completeness, authenticity, readability and retrievability. of the records.

In addition to the above, it is important to note that records control should also include defining requirements for record retention and disposition of records once they are no longer needed. The ISO/IEC 17025:2017 standard states that records must be retained for a specified period of time and must be securely and confidentially disposed of once they are no longer needed.

In summary, record control is a key requirement of ISO/IEC 17025:2017 and is essential to ensure traceability, proficiency and conformance in the testing and calibration process. It is important to establish an appropriate records control system that allows records to be created, maintained, accessed, and retrieved securely and confidentially, as well as to be retained and disposed of appropriately.

Here is a record control plan that can be used to implement ISO/IEC 17025:2017:

1. Identify the required records: The first stage in records control is to identify the records that are required to meet the requirements of ISO / IEC 17025:2017. These records may include test and calibration reports, equipment maintenance and calibration records, personnel training records, internal quality control records, and any other records required by the standard.

2. Establish the format and content of the records: Once the required records have been identified, the format and content of each record must be established. This may include establishing specific data fields, including identifying information, defining record numbering procedures, and defining record-keeping requirements.

3. Establish a records control system: After establishing the format and content of the records, a records control system must be established that allows proper tracking and maintenance of the records. This may include defining roles and responsibilities for record creation, maintenance, and control, implementing a record tracking and retrieval system, and defining record security and access requirements.

4. Implement Record Control System: Once the record control system has been established, it should be implemented and communicated to all personnel involved in performing tests and calibrations. This may include training staff in the use of the records control system and implementing an internal audit process to verify the effectiveness of the records control system.

5. Review and continual improvement: Finally, a process for review and continual improvement of the records control system must be established to ensure that it remains up-to-date and effective. This may include periodic review of the records control system and implementation of improvements in response to changes in the requirements of ISO /IEC 17025:2017 or feedback received from clients or auditors.

This records control plan can be adapted to meet the specific requirements of any organization seeking to implement ISO/IEC 17025:2017.

Some examples for record control in the ISO/IEC 17025:2017 standard:

1. Establishment of procedures for the creation, review, approval and distribution of records.

Example: The laboratory establishes a procedure for creating test and calibration reports that includes identification of items to include in the report, review and approval of the report by authorized personnel, and distribution of the report to customers and interested parties.

2. Assignment of clear responsibilities for the creation and maintenance of records.

Example: The laboratory assigns responsibility to a staff member for the creation and maintenance of personnel training records, including tracking training attendance and updating the records accordingly.

3. Definition of requirements for the retention and disposition of records.

Example: The laboratory establishes a five-year retention period for equipment calibration records, and defines a procedure for the secure and confidential deletion of the records after the retention period expires.

4. Establishment of security measures to protect the integrity and confidentiality of the records.

Example: The laboratory establishes security measures to protect the integrity and confidentiality of records, such as restricted access to records and protection against unauthorized tampering.

5. Implementation of a system for the recovery and access of records.

Example: The laboratory implements a document management system that allows retrieval and access of test and calibration records by date, lot number, customer, or any other relevant search criteria.

These are some examples of how record control can be implemented in the laboratory to meet the requirements of ISO/IEC 17025:2017. It is important that the laboratory has a systematic and documented approach to record control, and that records are managed effectively to ensure traceability, proficiency and compliance in the testing and calibration process.

In ISO/IEC 17025:2017, I can say that forms and records are two types of important documents in the context of an accredited laboratory. Although both are important for the documentation of laboratory activities and results, there are important differences between them.

A form is a document used to collect data or information in a structured and systematic way. For example, a form can be used to collect information about the identification of a sample, the analysis method to be used, the analysis conditions, etc. The forms can be used by laboratory personnel to document the results of a test, and they can also be used to provide information to customers and other stakeholders.

On the other hand, a record is a document that is used to document information about an activity, an event, or a result. The records can be used to document the actions of the laboratory in relation to compliance with ISO/IEC 17025:2017, including quality management, resource management, testing, results reporting, management of complaints and the control of non-conformities.

One important difference between forms and records is that forms are used to collect information while records are used to document information. Forms are typically used by laboratory personnel to collect data or information about an activity or result, while records are used to document the results of that activity or result.

Additionally, forms are typically living documents that are filled out and updated as lab activities are performed, while records are static documents that are used to document the final results of those activities.

Forms and records are two types of important documents in the context of an accredited laboratory, and they are used for different purposes. Forms are used to collect information, while records are used to document information. Forms are dynamic documents, while records are static documents.

9 PROCEDURES FOR RISK MANAGEMENT IN THE IMPLEMENTATION OF ISO/IEC 17025:2017 STANDARD

It is important to highlight that risk management is a key process in the implementation of the ISO/IEC 17025:2017 standard. The standard requires laboratories to identify and manage risks that may affect the quality of test results. Therefore, a well-developed risk management plan is essential to ensure the quality and accuracy of test results.

In addition, risk management must be an ongoing process. Risks can change over time, so it is important that laboratories regularly monitor and review their risk management plan to ensure it remains effective and appropriate for current circumstances.

It is also important to emphasize that risk management must be a process embedded in the culture of the organization. This means that it must be a collaborative and team approach, involving all members of the laboratory staff. All laboratory staff members must be trained in risk identification and management and be committed to the effective implementation of the risk management plan.

Finally, it is important to highlight that the risk management plan must be documented and maintained. Documentation may include the risk assessment matrix, mitigation measures, and any monitoring and reviews performed. This documentation can be useful during internal and external audits and reviews to demonstrate that the laboratory has implemented an effective risk management process.

A plan for risk management procedures in the implementation of ISO/IEC 17025:2017 is shared below. This plan can help laboratories assess and mitigate risks that may affect the quality of test results. The following are the steps for developing a risk management procedure:

1. Risk Identification: The first step in developing a risk management plan is to identify risks that may affect the quality of test results. Risks

can be internal (for example, human error, faulty equipment) or external (for example, changes in legal or regulatory requirements). An effective way to identify risks is to carry out a desk review and evaluation of laboratory processes and procedures.

2. Risk assessment: Once the risks have been identified, it is necessary to assess their probability and their potential impact. This can be done using a risk assessment matrix, where a score is assigned to the probability and impact of each risk. Risk assessment can help the laboratory to prioritize risks and determine what mitigation measures are necessary.

3. Risk mitigation: Once the risks have been assessed, the next step is to develop mitigation measures to reduce the likelihood and/or impact of the identified risks. These measures may include the implementation of additional quality controls, the training and training of personnel, the acquisition of more reliable equipment, the review and updating of procedures, among others.

4. Monitoring and review: Once mitigation measures are in place, it is important to regularly monitor and review the risk management plan to ensure that it remains effective and adapts to any changes in laboratory processes or regulatory requirements. Monitoring and review may include conducting internal audits and periodic reviews of procedures.

Some examples of risk management procedures in ISO/IEC 17025:2017:

• Hazard Identification: This procedure describes the process for identifying hazards that may affect the quality of test results. The laboratory can use tools such as the risk assessment matrix to identify and rank risks based on their potential impact.

• Risk Assessment: This procedure describes the process for assessing the likelihood and impact of each identified risk. Tools such as the Risk Assessment Matrix can be used by the laboratory to assess risks based on their likelihood and potential impact.

- Risk Mitigation: This procedure describes the process for implementing mitigation measures to reduce or eliminate identified risks. The laboratory may develop a risk mitigation plan that includes measures such as process change, implementation of additional controls, and personnel training.

- Monitoring and review: This procedure describes the process for monitoring and reviewing the risk management plan to ensure that it continues to be effective and appropriate for current circumstances. The laboratory may establish a regular review program to monitor and update the risk management plan as necessary.

- Communication and Consultation: This procedure describes the process for communicating and consulting with relevant interested parties on identified risks and implemented mitigation measures. The laboratory may establish a process for communication and consultation with customers, suppliers and other interested parties to ensure that risks are understood and mitigation measures implemented.

It is advisable to have a procedure that contains all the previous points well described.

10 CONTROLS OF PROCESSES AND SERVICES FOR THE TEST AND CALIBRATION OF MEASUREMENT EQUIPMENT

The control of processes and services for the testing and calibration of measurement equipment is one of the most critical aspects in the implementation of the ISO/IEC 17025:2017 standard. To ensure that the processes and services are carried out effectively and comply with the requirements of the standard, it is necessary to establish a control plan that includes a series of specific actions, as described below:

1. Identification of critical processes and services: First, the laboratory must identify the critical processes and services that are used for testing and calibrating the measurement equipment. These processes may include, for example, calibration of measurement equipment, sample preparation, data analysis, and interpretation of results.

2. Definition of acceptance criteria: It is important to define the acceptance criteria for each of the critical processes and services identified. These criteria may include, for example, precision, accuracy, repeatability, reproducibility, response time, and traceability.

3. Development of procedures: Documented procedures must be developed for each of the identified critical processes and services. These procedures must describe in detail the activities carried out in each process and service, including specific instructions for carrying out the tasks and the necessary quality controls.

4. Staff training: It is essential to train the staff who are involved in carrying out critical processes and services to ensure that they can carry out their tasks effectively. This includes training in documented procedures, acceptance criteria, and quality control techniques.

5. Monitoring and measurement: The laboratory must establish a monitoring and measurement plan for each of the critical processes and services identified. This involves carrying out periodic inspections to

ensure that processes and services are being carried out in accordance with documented procedures and that they meet defined acceptance criteria.

6. Corrective and preventive actions: If any deviation from the acceptance criteria is identified, the laboratory must take corrective and preventive actions. This may involve identifying the root cause of the problem and implementing measures to prevent a recurrence in the future.

7. Review and continuous improvement: Finally, it is important to periodically review processes and services to identify opportunities for improvement and make changes when necessary. This may include updating documented procedures and training personnel in new practices and techniques. In addition, it is important to carry out regular internal audits to ensure that the quality management system is being implemented effectively and that the requirements of ISO / IEC 17025:2017 are being met.

As examples of process control and services for the testing and calibration of measurement equipment within the framework of the ISO/IEC 17025:2017 standard, we can mention the following:

• Control of environmental conditions: it is necessary to ensure that the environmental conditions (temperature, humidity, lighting, etc.) are adequate to carry out the tests and calibrations in an accurate and reproducible manner. For this, procedures must be established for the monitoring and control of these conditions.

• Control of traceability: it is important that the measurement equipment used in the tests and calibrations are traced to reference standards established by accreditation bodies or recognized institutions. Procedures must be established to control and record the traceability of the equipment used.

• Personnel control: it is necessary that the personnel in charge of carrying out the tests and calibrations be duly trained and have the necessary experience to carry them out properly. Procedures must be established for the selection, training and evaluation of the personnel in charge of carrying out the tests and calibrations.

• Control of the equipment and materials used: it is necessary to ensure that the equipment and materials used in the tests and calibrations are in good condition and are appropriate for the intended purposes. Procedures must be established for the control, maintenance and calibration of the equipment used, as well as for the selection and evaluation of the materials used in the tests and calibrations.

• Control of procedures and records: it is important that the procedures used to carry out the tests and calibrations are properly documented and that a record of all the activities carried out is kept. Procedures should be established for the creation, review, approval, and distribution of procedures, as well as for the recording and archiving of related records and documentation.

11 ISO/IEC 17025:2017 STANDARD REQUIREMENTS FOR THE COMPETENCE OF LABORATORY PERSONNEL AND INFRASTRUCTURE

Establishing competency requirements for laboratory infrastructure and personnel is essential to comply with ISO /IEC 17025:2017. You need to assess your existing staff and infrastructure, develop education and training programs, identify the necessary infrastructure requirements, and document all requirements to ensure compliance and continual improvement.

The following is a plan to establish the requirements of ISO /IEC 17025:2017 for the competence of personnel and laboratory infrastructure:

1. Identification of competency requirements: A thorough review of the competency requirements for laboratory personnel and infrastructure established in ISO/ IEC 17025:2017 should be performed. This will make it possible to identify the key aspects that must be addressed to ensure compliance with these requirements.

2. Evaluation of the competence of the personnel: Procedures must be established to evaluate the competence of the personnel who work in the laboratory. This may include reviewing employees' resumes, experience and technical training, as well as conducting practical tests and periodic performance evaluations.

3. Development of education and training programs: Education and training programs should be developed for laboratory personnel in order to improve their technical competence and professional skills. These programs may include internal training courses, attendance at external courses, workshops and seminars, among others.

4. Evaluation and maintenance of laboratory infrastructure: Procedures must be established to evaluate and maintain laboratory infrastructure, including measurement equipment, facilities, and

environmental conditions. This may include the regular calibration and maintenance of equipment, the monitoring and control of environmental conditions, and the implementation of occupational health and safety measures.

5. Continuous review and improvement: Procedures must be established to periodically review the competence of laboratory personnel and infrastructure and to continuously improve processes and work practices to meet the requirements of ISO/IEC 17025: 2017.

6. Implementation of a quality management system: A quality management system based on ISO /IEC 17025:2017 must be implemented to ensure that the competence requirements of laboratory personnel and infrastructure are met. This may include creating a quality manual, documenting standard operating procedures, regularly reviewing quality records, and conducting internal and external audits to assess the performance of the quality management system.

7. Identification of Roles and Responsibilities: It is important to identify the roles and responsibilities of laboratory team members to ensure tasks are performed efficiently and competency requirements are met. This includes the identification of specific responsibilities for quality management, infrastructure management and personnel management.

8. Development of a human resources policy: A human resources policy should be developed that defines the competency and skill requirements for the different roles in the laboratory, including education, training and experience requirements. This policy may also include the definition of professional development programs for laboratory employees.

9. Identification of the infrastructure requirements: It is necessary to identify the infrastructure requirements necessary to carry out the tests and calibrations, including the space, equipment and material requirements necessary to guarantee the quality of the results.

10. Documentation of Requirements: Competence requirements for laboratory infrastructure and personnel must be documented in standard operating procedures and other relevant documentation. This will help ensure that the requirements are clearly understood and effectively met.

11. Personnel performance evaluation: Procedures must be established to evaluate the performance of laboratory personnel and establish personalized improvement plans to help employees improve their technical competence and professional skills.

12. Infrastructure maintenance and updating: Procedures must be established for the maintenance and updating of the laboratory infrastructure, including preventive and corrective maintenance of the equipment and the planning of updates and improvements.

Some tips to improve the plan for establishing the requirements of the ISO /IEC 17025:2017 standard for the competence of personnel and laboratory infrastructure:

• Identify and prioritize risks: Identify the risks and opportunities associated with meeting laboratory infrastructure and personnel competency requirements, and prioritize them to ensure those with the greatest impact are addressed first.

• Foster communication and collaboration: Foster communication and collaboration between laboratory staff and other team members, as well as with clients and other stakeholders, to ensure that competency requirements are met and any issues are addressed. timely.

• Promote continuous education: Encourage the training and continuous development of laboratory personnel to ensure that they are up to date with the latest technologies and methodologies, and that they have the necessary skills to carry out their work effectively.

• Carry out regular internal audits: Carry out regular internal audits to assess the effectiveness of established procedures and to identify areas for improvement.

• Carry out management reviews: Carry out periodic management reviews to assess the effectiveness of the plan for establishing the requirements of ISO /IEC 17025:2017 for the competence of personnel and laboratory infrastructure, and to identify any changes that should be done to improve compliance and quality of results.

• Securing customer feedback: Securing customer feedback and considering their comments when establishing competency requirements for laboratory infrastructure and personnel, to ensure that their expectations and needs are being met.

12 INTERNAL AUDITS OF THE QUALITY MANAGEMENT SYSTEM

A good internal audit plan of the quality management system to meet the requirements of ISO/IEC 17025:2017 is:

1. Establish the scope of the audit: Determine the scope of the internal audit, which implies identifying the areas of the quality management system that will be evaluated.

2. Select the audit team: Select a team of internal auditors with adequate experience and skills to carry out the audit. The team must be independent of the area being audited and must not have a conflict of interest.

3. Plan the audit: Establish an audit plan, including the schedule, objectives, audit criteria, audit methods, necessary resources, and required documentation.

4. Carry out the audit: Carry out the internal audit according to the established plan, reviewing the documentation, interviewing the personnel and making on-site observations.

5. Identify non-conformities: Identify and record any non-conformities found during the audit, as well as any positive findings or potential improvements.

6. Report audit results: Present the audit results to relevant laboratory personnel, including management, for review and action.

7. Take corrective action: Take corrective action to address nonconformities identified during the internal audit, including assigning responsibilities, deadlines, and follow-up actions.

8. Follow Up: Track corrective actions taken to ensure that they have been completed and have been effective.

9. Continuous improvement: Use the results of the internal audit as part of the process of continuous improvement of the quality management system, to identify opportunities for improvement and strengthen the positive aspects of the system.

Some additional points to keep in mind are:

• Consider audit team rotation: To avoid complacency and loss of objectivity, it is important that audit team members are rotated regularly.

• Establish a feedback system: It is important to establish a feedback system that allows auditors and assessed personnel to provide feedback on the audit process and any areas that can be improved.

• Consider customer feedback: In addition to evaluating the internal quality management system, it is important to consider feedback from external customers to ensure that the laboratory is meeting their expectations and requirements.

• Be objective and impartial: Internal auditors must be objective and impartial when evaluating the quality management system. They must base their conclusions and recommendations on factual evidence and not on personal opinion.

• Comply with legal and regulatory requirements: In addition to complying with the requirements of ISO /IEC 17025:2017, it is important to ensure that you comply with all relevant legal and regulatory requirements.

• Schedule regular audits: It is advisable to schedule regular audits to ensure that the quality management system remains in line with the requirements of ISO / IEC 17025:2017 and that non-conformities identified in previous audits are addressed.

By following these points, a more effective internal audit of the quality management system can be carried out and ensure that all the requirements of ISO/IEC 17025:2017 are met.

13 PERIODIC MANAGEMENT REVIEW FOR THE IMPLEMENTATION OF ISO/IEC 17025:2017 STANDARD

The periodic management review is an important activity in the quality management system, since it allows the top management of the organization to evaluate the performance of the system and make strategic decisions to improve it. In the case of the implementation of ISO/IEC 17025:2017, it is necessary to establish a plan to carry out these reviews effectively.

A periodic management review plan for the effective implementation of ISO/IEC 17025:2017 is:

1. Establish a schedule: Determine how often periodic management reviews will take place. The ISO /IEC 17025:2017 standard recommends that a review be carried out at least once a year.

2. Appoint a review team: Select a review team that includes key representatives from the lab. The team should be made up of people with relevant experience and knowledge, and they should be in a position to make strategic decisions.

3. Reporting: Prepare review reports that summarize the main results, trends and conclusions of the evaluation of the quality management system. Reports should include an evaluation of the laboratory's performance, an assessment of opportunities for improvement, and an action plan to address areas that need improvement.

4. Review of the quality management system: Management shall review the quality management system to ensure that it continues to be effective and fit for purpose. The review should cover all elements of the quality management system, including the quality policy, quality objectives and documented processes.

5. Identification of improvements: The review team must identify opportunities for improvement and suggest corrective and preventive actions to address deficiencies. This may include updating procedures,

providing more staff training, or investing in new technology or equipment.

6. Implementation of Improvements: Once improvement opportunities have been identified, the review team must establish an action plan and timetable for implementing the improvements. Progress should be monitored and reported at the following year's periodic management review.

The periodic management review should include the following elements:

• Frequency: It is important to establish how often the management review will take place. This may depend on the complexity of the quality management system, the size of the organization, the number of laboratories involved, and other relevant factors. The ISO /IEC 17025:2017 standard suggests an annual review, but this can be adjusted according to the specific needs of the organization.

• Issues to be covered: It is necessary to establish the issues that will be addressed in the management review. These may include the performance of the quality management system, the effectiveness of corrective and preventive actions, customer satisfaction, the performance of laboratories, the performance of personnel, among others.

• Required Documentation: It is important to establish what documentation is required for management review. This may include internal audit reports, nonconformity and corrective action reports, staff performance reports, and other relevant documents.

• Responsibilities and roles: It are necessary to establish who will be responsible for carrying out the management review and what roles they will play. For example, the quality manager may lead the management review, while laboratory managers may provide feedback on laboratory performance.

• Follow-up actions: After the management review, it is important to establish follow-up actions to ensure that the decisions made are correctly implemented. This can include the assignment of specific tasks to individuals or teams and the definition of deadlines for the implementation of actions.

The plan for periodic management review is an important element to ensure the effective implementation of ISO/IEC 17025:2017. The periodic review will allow the top management of the organization to evaluate the performance of the quality management system, make strategic decisions to improve it and ensure its continuous effectiveness.

14 CONTINUOUS IMPROVEMENTS OF THE QUALITY MANAGEMENT SYSTEM

Once the areas for improvement have been identified and the specific objectives have been established, it is important to establish a detailed action plan to achieve the objectives. This plan must be realistic and feasible, and must include specific activities, deadlines, responsibilities and resources necessary to carry out the actions.

It is advisable to involve all laboratory personnel in the continuous improvement process, as this will increase the probability of success of the plan. In addition, it is important to assign clear responsibilities to each staff member to ensure that the actions and deadlines set out in the plan are met.

To implement the action plan, it may be necessary to provide training to laboratory personnel in new techniques, procedures, and protocols. Additionally, it may be necessary to update existing procedures to ensure that new improvement requirements are met.

Once the actions have been implemented, it is important to carry out follow-up and monitoring to ensure that they are being carried out effectively and the established improvement objectives are being achieved. This monitoring may include measuring and analyzing the results, identifying the causes of any problems, and taking corrective action to fix them.

Finally, it is important to evaluate the results obtained from the implemented actions and compare them with the established objectives. If the results are satisfactory, they must be maintained and continually improved. If the objectives are not reached, the causes must be identified and new actions established to achieve them.

A good plan for the continuous improvement of the quality management system in a laboratory consists of the following steps:

1. Identify areas for improvement: The first thing to do is identify the areas for improvement in the laboratory. For this, an internal evaluation

or an audit can be carried out to detect the strengths and weaknesses of the quality management system.

2. Establish improvement objectives: Once the areas for improvement have been identified, specific objectives must be established for each of them. These objectives must be measurable, achievable, relevant and aimed at continuous improvement.

3. Establish an action plan: To achieve the improvement objectives, a detailed action plan must be established that includes specific activities, deadlines, responsibilities and resources necessary to carry out the actions.

4. Implement the action plan: Once the action plan is established, it must be implemented in the laboratory. This may require staff training, updating of procedures, and the allocation of resources.

5. Follow up and monitor: It is important to follow up and monitor the actions implemented to ensure that they are being carried out effectively and the established improvement objectives are being achieved.

6. Evaluate the results: Finally, the results obtained from the implemented actions must be evaluated and compared with the established objectives. If the results are satisfactory, they must be maintained and continually improved. If the objectives are not reached, the causes must be identified and new actions established to achieve them.

The continuous improvement of the quality management system in a laboratory implies a systematic and proactive approach to the identification and resolution of problems, with the aim of continuously improving the efficiency of the laboratory. This requires the active participation of all laboratory personnel, and a disciplined and rigorous approach to the implementation of actions and the follow-up and monitoring of results.

15 PREPARING FOR THE ISO/IEC 17025:2017 ACCREDITATION ASSESSMENT

Preparation for the ISO/IEC 17025:2017 accreditation assessment involves becoming familiar with the standard, having adequate documentation of the quality management system, identifying gaps and planning its implementation, assessing the technical competence of personnel, establishing a management system quality control, conduct internal audits and prepare for external evaluation. Compliance with the requirements of ISO/IEC 17025:2017 can help the laboratory improve the quality of its results and maintain the trust of its customers and interested parties.

A plan for preparing for accreditation evaluation consists of the following steps:

1. Familiarization with ISO /IEC 17025:2017: It is important that laboratory personnel, particularly those involved in quality management, become familiar with ISO/IEC 17025:2017. This will help ensure that the laboratory meets the requirements of the standard during the accreditation evaluation.

2. Documentation of the quality management system: The laboratory must have adequate documentation of its quality management system to demonstrate compliance with the requirements of ISO /IEC 17025:2017. This includes a quality policy, standard operating procedures, quality records, and other relevant documents.

3. Identification of gaps and implementation planning: The internal assessment should identify any gaps in the laboratory's quality management system and a detailed plan should be created to address these gaps. This plan should include timelines, responsibilities, and resources needed for implementation.

4. Assessment of the technical competence of the personnel: The accreditation evaluators will also evaluate the technical competence of the laboratory personnel. It is important that the laboratory has a

training and training plan to ensure that the staff have the necessary skills and knowledge to perform their tasks.

5. Establishment of an effective quality management system: An effective quality management system is essential to meet the requirements of ISO / IEC 17025:2017. The laboratory must have a documented quality management system and apply continuous improvement processes to guarantee the quality of its results.

6. Internal audit: Internal audit is an important tool to ensure that the laboratory's quality management system meets the requirements of ISO / IEC 17025:2017. Internal audit can also help identify opportunities for improvement.

7. Preparation for external evaluation: The laboratory must ensure that it is prepared for external evaluation by the accreditation body. This includes preparing the necessary documentation, making resources and staff available, and conducting assessment drills to ensure that all staff are familiar with the assessment process.

8. Continuous evaluation and review: After the external evaluation, it is important to carry out a continuous review and evaluation of the quality management system of the laboratory to ensure that it continues to comply with the requirements of ISO / IEC 17025:2017.

Finally, we can summarize that to obtain the ISO/IEC 17025:2017 accreditation, the following general steps must be followed:

• Identify the requirements of the standard: It is important that the laboratory knows all the requirements of the ISO /IEC 17025:2017 standard and has an action plan to comply with them.

• Carry out a self-assessment: The laboratory must carry out a self-assessment to identify areas for improvement and establish an action plan.

• Implement a quality management system: The laboratory must implement a quality management system that meets the requirements of ISO / IEC 17025:2017.

• Prepare the necessary documentation: The laboratory must prepare the necessary documentation to demonstrate compliance with the requirements of the standard.

• Carry out internal audits: The laboratory must carry out internal audits to ensure that its quality management system is working correctly and complying with the requirements of the standard.

• Carry out the certification audit: An accredited certification body will carry out a certification audit to assess whether the laboratory complies with the requirements of the standard.

• Obtain accreditation: If the laboratory meets the requirements of the standard, it will receive ISO /IEC 17025:2017 accreditation.

It is important to highlight that the process of obtaining ISO/IEC 17025:2017 accreditation can be long and expensive, but it is essential to demonstrate the technical competence and the quality of the services offered by the laboratory.

16 CONCLUSIONS

In conclusion, the ISO/IEC 17025:2017 standard is a solid and stable framework for quality management in laboratories. The implementation of the standard allows laboratories to ensure that their results are accurate, reliable and reproducible, and that they meet the expectations of their customers and interested parties.

ISO/IEC 17025:2017 also provides a risk-based and systematic approach to quality management, enabling laboratories to identify and address continuous improvement opportunities. Continual improvement is a key component of ISO/IEC 17025:2017, and laboratories are encouraged to look for opportunities to continuously improve their processes and results.

The ISO/IEC 17025:2017 standard is a powerful tool for laboratories that want to improve the quality of their results and the satisfaction of their customers and stakeholders. Implementing the standard not only enables laboratories to meet accreditation and regulatory requirements, but also helps establish a culture of continuous improvement throughout the laboratory.

In addition to the above mentioned, I would like to emphasize the importance of risk management in ISO/IEC 17025:2017. Risk management is essential to ensure that laboratories identify and address potential risks that may affect the quality and accuracy of their results. Risk identification and management are continuous processes and must be integrated into all laboratory operations.

It is also important to note that ISO/IEC 17025:2017 applies to all types of laboratories, whether they are in the public or private sector, industry or academia. The standard focuses on technical competence and the ability of the laboratory to produce accurate and reliable results, regardless of its location or type of laboratory.

Another key aspect of ISO/IEC 17025:2017 is the importance placed on the training and competence of laboratory personnel. The standard requires that laboratories have a personnel competency management system, which includes the evaluation and continuous monitoring of personnel performance. In addition, laboratories must provide ongoing training to their staff to ensure they are up to date with the latest technologies, techniques, and industry standards.

In summary, the ISO/IEC 17025:2017 standard is a robust and effective framework for quality management in laboratories. Implementation of the standard helps laboratories improve the accuracy and reliability of their results, meet accreditation and regulatory requirements, and establish a culture of continuous improvement throughout the laboratory. Risk management, training and competence of personnel are critical aspects to consider when implementing ISO/IEC 17025:2017.

We hope this book has been useful to those looking to implement ISO/IEC 17025:2017 or improve their quality management systems in existing laboratories. We wish you all much success on your journey towards excellence in laboratory quality management.

For more information you can go to www.rodspa.com.

17 BIBLIOGRAPHY

- "ISO/IEC 17025:2017: General requirements for the competence of testing and calibration laboratories" of the International Organization for Standardization (ISO).

This is the official standard for ISO/IEC 17025:2017 and provides the general requirements for the technical competence and quality management of laboratories. It is an essential resource for understanding the requirements of the standard and how to implement them.

- "Implementing ISO/IEC 17025:2017: A Practical Guide" by Baskar Kotte.

This book provides a practical and detailed guide on how to implement ISO/IEC 17025:2017 in a laboratory. Includes examples and case studies to illustrate concepts and best practices.

- "ISO/IEC 17025:2017: The Complete Guide to Laboratory Accreditation and Certification" by Perry Johnson Laboratory Accreditation, Inc.

This book is a complete guide on laboratory accreditation and certification according to ISO/IEC 17025:2017. It provides detailed information on accreditation requirements, audit and assessment processes, and best practices for complying with the standard.

- "ISO/IEC 17025 Quality Manual Template" by Bizmanualz, Inc.

This resource provides an ISO/IEC 17025:2017 quality manual template to help laboratories implement the standard more efficiently. Includes sections and examples to guide the creation of a custom quality manual.

- "ISO/IEC 17025:2017 - Understanding and Implementing" by Infinium Global Research.

This book provides an overview of ISO/IEC 17025:2017 and its implementation in laboratories. Includes case studies and tips for meeting the standard's requirements and achieving accreditation.

These are just a few bibliography suggestions. There are many other resources available online and in specialized bookstores that can be useful for implementing ISO/IEC 17025:2017 in a laboratory.

For more information you can go to www.rodspa.com

GLOSSARY

- Accreditation: process by which an accreditation body formally recognizes the technical competence of a laboratory to carry out specific tests or calibrations.
- Calibration: process by which the relationship between the measurement values indicated by a measurement instrument and the corresponding values of a reference standard is established.
- Competence: ability to apply knowledge and skills to achieve desired results.
- Test: determination of one or more characteristics of an object or of a test sample according to an established procedure.
- Test and calibration equipment: any equipment used to carry out tests or calibrations, including measurement equipment and support equipment.
- Measurement uncertainty: parameter that characterizes the dispersion of the values attributed to a measurand, based on the information used.
- Laboratory: organization or part of an organization that performs tests or calibrations.
- Test or calibration method: procedure for carrying out a test or calibration.
- Technical personnel: personnel who have the necessary training, experience and knowledge to carry out tests or calibrations and to evaluate the results.
- Procedure: description of the activities necessary to carry out a test or calibration.
- Method validation: process by which the ability of the method to produce valid results for a given set of samples is checked.
- Method verification: process by which it is verified that the method is capable of producing valid results for the specific conditions of use.

These are just some of the more commonly used terms in ISO/IEC 17025:2017. It is important that users of the standard become familiar with and fully understand these terms to ensure proper implementation of the standard in their laboratories.

ABOUT THE AUTHOR

Rodrigo Palma Mena is an advisor born in Santiago de Chile in 1977. He is known for advising chemical laboratories for the implementation of the ISO/IEC 17025:2017 standard, for teaching standard courses that are requested by the accreditation body in Chile, as well as preparing quality managers and auditing to carry out the diagnosis of the laboratories. In addition to his advisory career, he has worked as a chemist and QA/QC engineer in different laboratories in different areas such as pharmaceuticals, raw materials, pesticides, herbicides, clinical and mining. He has more than 19 years of experience related to the standard and lived through the process of updating the standard in 2017.

For more information you can go to www.rodspa.com[1]

---

1.   http://www.rodspa.com

"Excellence in quality management is not a destination, it is a journey. A journey that requires commitment, dedication and the constant search for continuous improvement. It is a journey that leads us to excellence in customer satisfaction, in the process efficiency and market competitiveness. It is a journey that leads us to be leaders in our sector and make a difference. But, above all, it is a journey that leads us to improve people's lives, offering products and services of the highest quality and reliability".

Don't miss out!

Visit the website below and you can sign up to receive emails whenever Rodrigo Palma publishes a new book. There's no charge and no obligation.

https://books2read.com/r/B-A-IDRIB-RARDD

BOOKS 2 READ

Connecting independent readers to independent writers.

Also by Rodrigo Palma

El Arte de Guiar desde Adentro: Estrategias para Desarrollar tu
Liderazgo Personal
ISO/IEC 17025:2017 and the success of the laboratory: a guide for
implementation
ISO/IEC 17025:2017 y el éxito del laboratorio: una guía para la
implementación
The Art of Leading from Within: Strategies to Develop Your Personal
Leadership

www.ingramcontent.com/pod-product-compliance
Lightning Source LLC
Chambersburg PA
CBHW052230150726

48002CB00003B/1357